FIGURATIVELY SPEAKING

UNDERSTANDING
SAYINGS

BY
ROBIN JOHNSON

Crabtree Publishing Company

www.crabtreebooks.com

Crabtree Publishing Company

www.crabtreebooks.com

Author: Robin Johnson

**Publishing plan research
and development:** Reagan Miller

Photo research: Margaret Amy Salter

Editorial director: Kathy Middleton

Editor: Anastasia Suen

Proofreader and indexer: Wendy Scavuzzo

Cover design and logo: Margaret Amy Salter

**Layout, production coordinator and prepress
technician:** Margaret Amy Salter

Print coordinator: Margaret Amy Salter

Photographs:
All images by Shutterstock

Sayings featured on cover:

Middle left: Don't open up a can of worms! (Don't do something that you know will cause trouble.)

Middle right: He's no spring chicken. (He's not very young.)

Bottom: It's raining cats and dogs! (It's raining really hard.)

Library and Archives Canada Cataloguing in Publication

Johnson, Robin (Robin R.), author
        Understanding sayings / Robin Johnson.

(Figuratively speaking)
Includes index.
Issued in print and electronic formats.
ISBN 978-0-7787-1778-2 (bound).--ISBN 978-0-7787-1878-9
(paperback).--
ISBN 978-1-4271-1619-2 (pdf).--ISBN 978-1-4271-1615-4 (html)

        1. Idioms--Juvenile literature. 2. Proverbs--Juvenile literature.
I. Title.

P301.5.I34J64 2015   j418   C2015-903982-7
                                             C2015-903983-5

Library of Congress Cataloging-in-Publication Data

Johnson, Robin (Robin R.) author.
 Understanding sayings / Robin Johnson.
      pages cm. -- (Figuratively Speaking)
 Includes index.
 ISBN 978-0-7787-1778-2 (reinforced library binding : alk. paper)
-- ISBN 978-0-7787-1878-9 (pbk. : alk. paper) --
ISBN 978-1-4271-1619-2 (electronic pdf : alk. paper) --
ISBN 978-1-4271-1615-4 (electronic html : alk. paper)
 1. Idioms--Juvenile literature. 2. Figures of speech in literature--
Juvenile literature. I. Title.

 P301.5.I34J64 2015
 428--dc23

                        2015034436

Crabtree Publishing Company

www.crabtreebooks.com   1-800-387-7650

Printed in Canada/112015/EF20150911

Published in Canada
Crabtree Publishing
616 Welland Ave.
St. Catharines, ON
L2M 5V6

Published in the United States
Crabtree Publishing
PMB 59051
350 Fifth Avenue, 59th Floor
New York, New York 10118

Published in the United Kingdom
Crabtree Publishing
Maritime House
Basin Road North, Hove
BN41 1WR

Published in Australia
Crabtree Publishing
3 Charles Street
Coburg North
VIC, 3058

CONTENTS

What are sayings?.............. 4

Why use sayings?.............. 6

Sayings in pictures.............. 8

Sayings in stories...............12

Sayings in fairy tales............16

Sayings in fables................20

Sayings in myths 24

Revise your work................28

Publish your work..............30

Learning more..................31

Glossary and Index............32

WHAT ARE SAYINGS?

Did you wake up on the wrong side of the bed today? Maybe you were under the weather and wanted to take cover under the covers. But you had to get cracking and have a bite to eat. You spilled your milk, but there was no use crying over it. After breakfast, you had egg on your face and your hair was as flat as a pancake. But you had to shake a leg and head to school. You were tickled pink to sport your new sneakers. Then you bombed on your test and were down in the dumps again.

Does that sound like a normal day or does it just sound confusing? Those sentences are stuffed to the gills with **sayings**. A saying is a short, well-known statement that is used often. There is more to sayings than meets the eye, however. Let's take a look at the saying "tickled pink." You know how it feels to be tickled. You know what the color pink looks like. But did you know that "tickled pink" means to be very pleased? Keep reading to learn more sayings. You'll be tickled pink that you did!

FIGURATIVE OR LITERAL?

We use two types of language to tell our stories. We use **literal language** to state facts or describe things as they really are. If we say that Gabby spilled the beans all over the table, we mean she literally, or actually, knocked over a can of beans and they spilled. Oh dear!

We use **figurative language** to paint pictures with our words. Figurative language uses words or sayings with different meanings than their usual, literal meanings. If we say that Gabby spilled the beans about the surprise party, that doesn't mean she poured beans all over the party guests. "Spilled the beans" is a saying that means to give away a secret or surprise.

The **context** of a phrase will help you decide if it has a literal or figurative meaning. Context is all the surrounding words that help explain the meaning of a word or phrase. Read the sentences below. Notice the context clues that help you understand the phrase "in the doghouse."

LITERAL

"Fido has slept in the doghouse ever since he was a puppy."

This sentence is literal because Fido is a dog and he sleeps in a real doghouse.

FIGURATIVE

"Dad was in the doghouse when he forgot Mom's birthday."

This sentence is figurative because Dad did not really sleep in a doghouse—although Mom may have wanted him to. "In the doghouse" is a saying that means someone is unhappy with you.

WHY USE SAYINGS?

Sayings let you tell your stories in clever or colorful ways. Your **characters** can talk turkey (say what they really mean) or talk a blue streak (talk nonstop). They can walk on thin ice (be close to danger) or go the extra mile (go beyond what is asked of them). They can live on the edge (take risks) or live in glass houses (make themselves an easy target for criticism). Sayings make your stories and characters come alive.

There are more sayings than you can shake a stick at! In this book, you'll learn some **idioms**, **adages**, and **proverbs**. An idiom is a group of words that take on a special meaning when they're used together. "Out of the blue" (unexpectedly) and "be in the same boat" (share the same experience) are idioms. An adage is an old, well-known saying that expresses something most people think is true. "Where there's smoke, there's fire" is an adage which means if a rumor is going around there is usually some reason for it. A proverb is a short, clever saying that states a general truth or gives advice on how to act. "Practice makes perfect" is a proverb.

WRITE ON!

The pen is mightier than the sword! That saying means that words are powerful. Your writing can build bridges—or it can burn bridges. Your words can move mountains—or they can make mountains out of molehills. So put pen to paper and set the world on fire!

ABOUT THIS BOOK

Can't make heads or tails of all this? This book is divided into four sections to help you make sense of sayings.

FIGURE IT OUT! Explains how sayings show up in different types of writing.

TALK ABOUT IT! Shows you how to brainstorm and use tools to start the writing process.

WRITE ABOUT IT! Features samples and tips to help you write your own super stories.

NOW IT'S YOUR TURN! Encourages you to step up and create original work.

FIVE STEPS TO WRITING

1. PRE-WRITING: Put on your thinking cap and start brainstorming ideas.

2. DRAFTING: Get the ball rolling—and your pencil moving. Write your first copy and don't be a copycat!

3. REVISING: Rewrite and improve your work. Make a change—or two—for the better.

4. EDITING: Check for spelling, grammar, and punctuation errors. Make your writing as right as rain.

5. PUBLISHING: Share your good work with your family and friends. They will be all ears!

SAYINGS IN PICTURES

Sayings can be hard to understand. In fact, some sayings may seem to make no sense at all! Why do the idioms "slim chance" and "fat chance" mean the same thing? How can an easy task be both "a breeze" and "a piece of cake"? We can **visualize** sayings to help us understand them. To visualize is to make a picture in your head. Picture the literal meaning of a saying first. Then try to figure out the figurative meaning.

Look at the pictures below. Each one shows the literal meaning of a well-known saying involving animals. Try to guess the sayings they represent. It's anybody's guess! Then use clues in the artwork to figure out the figurative meaning of each saying.

PICTURE THIS
We say that a picture is worth a thousand words. That means you can get a lot of information from a simple picture. What important details do these cartoons show?

Worms

FIGURE IT OUT!

Did you get the picture and guess the meaning of each cartoon? Read the text below to check your answers.

OPEN A CAN OF WORMS

The man in this picture has literally opened a can of worms. Maybe he thought it was a can of beans or something else. At least he didn't spill the beans! But now the can is open and the worms are about to worm their way out of it. They will be hard to catch and will cause all sorts of mischief. So the saying "to open a can of worms" means to do something that will cause trouble.

WHEN PIGS FLY

Have you ever seen a pig with wings? Were you pigging out on a ham sandwich when you noticed a hog hamming it up in the air? No! Pigs can't fly, of course! So the saying "when pigs fly" means that something will never happen.

RAINING CATS AND DOGS

Cats and dogs don't really fall from the sky. But if they did, the weather would be *purrrfectly* awful. Everyone and their dog would carry umbrellas. There would be scaredy-cats running for cover like the boy in the picture. We say it's "raining cats and dogs" when it's raining really hard.

ANTS IN YOUR PANTS

Imagine you had an army of ants in your pants. You would squirm and wiggle like the boy in the picture. You would jump at the chance to get rid of those ants. We use the saying "ants in your pants" to describe someone who can't sit still. You might have ants in your pants if you are nervous about a test or excited to open a present.

Drew was wild about sayings, so he decided to draw his own animal cartoon. He brainstormed some sayings he had heard before and wrote them in a list. He looked up the meaning of each one to see which one would work best for his cartoon.

let the cat out of the bag

have a frog in your throat

a wolf in sheep's clothing

the cat's got your tongue

don't look a gift horse in the mouth

a horse of a different color

let sleeping dogs lie

pull a rabbit out of a hat

the elephant in the room

fight like cats and dogs

monkey business

the straw that broke the camel's back

hold your horses

WRITE ABOUT IT!

Drew picked the saying "a wolf in sheep's clothing" for his cartoon. He drew his picture in two shakes of a lamb's tail. Then he used the cartoon to guess the figurative meaning of the saying.

A WOLF IN SHEEP'S CLOTHING

A wolf is a wild animal that hunts sheep, deer, and other large animals. A sheep is a tame animal that is raised for its wool. People use the wool to make sweaters and other clothing. If a wolf wears a nice wool sweater or some woolen mittens, maybe it wants to stop hunting and be friends with the sheep. The wolf is dressed for success—instead of being dressed to kill. So the saying "a wolf in sheep's clothing" might describe someone who wants to act better, dress nicely, and make new friends.

DID DREW GET IT RIGHT?

"A wolf in sheep's clothing" is a dangerous person who pretends to be harmless.

NOW IT'S YOUR TURN!

Now it's your turn to get the picture! Pick a saying on the opposite page or use another one you know. Draw a cartoon that shows the literal meaning of the saying. Make it pretty as a picture! Then guess what the figurative meaning might be. Don't worry if you get it wrong (like Drew did). A saying can be a tough nut to crack!

SAYINGS IN STORIES

Many sayings start out in stories. Has anyone ever called you a goody two-shoes? It doesn't mean you have good-looking shoes! It means you always follow the rules and act very proper. The saying comes from an old children's story called "The History of Little Goody Two-Shoes." In the story, a poor orphan girl gets a new pair of shoes and shows them to everyone she meets. Over time, her nickname—Goody Two-Shoes—became an insulting idiom.

In *The Wonderful Wizard of Oz*, a girl named Dorothy gets a new pair of shoes, too. All she has to do to return home is click the heels of her shoes together. In this passage from the **novel**, Dorothy explains why she wants to leave the wonderful Land of Oz.

"Tell me something about yourself and the country you came from," said the Scarecrow, when she had finished her dinner. So she told him all about Kansas, and how gray everything was there, and how the cyclone had carried her to this [strange] Land of Oz.

The Scarecrow listened carefully, and said, "I cannot understand why you should wish to leave this beautiful country and go back to the dry, gray place you call Kansas."

"That is because you have no brains," answered the girl. "No matter how dreary and gray our homes are, we people of flesh and blood would rather live there than in any other country, be it ever so beautiful. There is no place like home."
—Excerpt from *The Wonderful Wizard of Oz* by L. Frank Baum

In the story, Dorothy lives in a small gray house with her gray-cheeked aunt and her gray-bearded uncle. Their house is gray. The plowed land on their farm is gray. Even the grass has been burned gray by the hot Kansas sun. Kansas is a farming state in the midwestern United States. It is known for having flat land, plentiful crops—and wild windstorms. Dorothy and her dog are swept up in a swirling tornado (also called a cyclone) and taken to a colorful land called Oz.

In another part of the novel, the writer describes Dorothy's arrival in Oz. He writes, "The cyclone had set the house down very gently—for a cyclone—in the midst of a country of marvelous beauty. There were lovely patches of [green grass] all about, with stately trees bearing rich and luscious fruits. Banks of gorgeous flowers were on every hand, and birds with rare and brilliant plumage sang and fluttered in the trees and bushes. A little way off was a small brook, rushing and sparkling along between green banks, and murmuring in a voice very grateful to a little girl who had lived so long on the dry, gray prairies."

Dorothy marvels at the wonders of Oz. But she never stops missing her home or trying to get back there. Throughout the novel, she meets colorful characters, makes new friends, and has exciting adventures. She also learns that beauty is only skin deep, for there is evil lurking in the lovely Land of Oz. Dorothy's home may be "dreary and gray," but it's where her heart is. Her exclamation, "There is no place like home," has become a familiar saying for anyone expressing joy at coming home.

Why do you think Dorothy wants to go home? What makes your home special?

Cassie was feeling at home with sayings, so she decided to use one for her story. She brainstormed some home-style sayings.

keep the home fires burning

home sweet home

east, west, home's best

in the home stretch

hit a home run

home away from home

until the cows come home

make yourself at home

bring home the bacon

home is where the heart is

your home is your castle

Cassie decided to use the saying "until the cows come home" to write a *mooooving* story about some cows. She added characters and **dialogue** to beef it up. Cassie underlined all the sayings in her story. Do some research yourself to find out what each one means.

One day, some curious cows wondered if <u>the grass was greener on the other side</u> of the fence. So they <u>got up with the chickens</u>, and set out for <u>greener pastures</u>. They had been gone a very long time, when the other animals began to stew. They knew the farmer would not feed them <u>until the cows came home</u>.

"I'm <u>hungry as a horse!</u>" neighed a horse.
"Me, too!" oinked a pig, who always <u>ate like a pig</u>.
"Those cows really <u>get my goat!</u>" bleated a goat.
"<u>Don't have a cow!</u>" said a sheep. "Those cows will be baaaack soon. You can <u>bet the farm on it!</u>"

Just then, the animals spotted the cows. They were on their way back and had smiles as <u>broad as a barn door</u>. They had left the farm <u>with bells on</u>. But now they knew <u>there was no place like home</u>.

Now it's your turn to make yourself at home! Pick a homey saying and use it to write a short story. Tell the tale of a pig who brings home the bacon. Write a home-sweet-home story about a candy house. Hit a home run with a sporty story. Choose your saying and make your story something to write home about!

SAYINGS IN FAIRY TALES

Do you think **fairy tales** are fairly silly or just for little kids? Well, don't judge a book by its cover! We can all learn a thing or two from fairy tales. "Rapunzel" teaches us to let our hair down once in a while. "Jack and the Beanstalk" warns us not to kill the goose that lays the golden egg. The passage below from "Cinderella" shows us that if the shoe fits, wear it!

The next day the King sent out all his heralds and trumpeters with a Proclamation, saying that the Prince would marry the lady whose foot the slipper fitted. But though all the ladies in the land tried on the slipper it would fit none of them—their feet were all too big!

At last the heralds came to the house where Cinderella lived. The eldest stepsister tried the slipper on first, but it was quite impossible for her to get her foot into it, for her great toe was too big... The slipper would not fit, and at last she was obliged to hand it to her sister.

But the other sister had no better luck. She did, indeed, get her toes inside, but her foot was much too long, and her heel stuck out behind... She, too, had to give up the attempt to force her foot into it.

Then Cinderella came shyly out from behind the door where she had been standing out of sight, and asked if she might try on the slipper... And it fitted her exactly!

...The Prince was overjoyed to find her again; and they were married at once with much pomp amid great rejoicings.
—Excerpt from "The Story of Cinderella" by Logan Marshall

A fairy tale is a short children's story about magical beings and lands. The term "fairy tale" is also an idiom for a false story or lie meant to trick people.

This fairy tale is full of sayings. In fact, the term "Cinderella story" is an idiom itself! It's used to describe something good happening to someone poor or nice. "Cinderella" is the story of a poor, sweet girl whose wicked stepmother and stepsisters work her to the bone. One day, a handsome prince invites all the young women in the land to a fancy ball. A kind Fairy Godmother visits Cinderella and changes her rags into a beautiful gown. Cinderella goes to the castle and has a ball— but only until midnight, when the magic spell wears off. Then she runs from the prince, leaving a glass slipper behind her. The prince uses the shoe to find his perfect mate.

In the passage from the story, the prince's footmen search the land to find the right foot—which is quite a feat! The stepsisters try to squeeze their big feet into the little glass slipper. But the cruel sisters can't "put themselves in someone else's shoes." That saying means to understand another person's feelings and see their point of view. Cinderella puts her best foot forward and the shoe fits. Luckily she doesn't have two left feet! Then she and the prince start their life together—on the right foot.

The Cinderella story gives us some rich sayings. The prince hosts a ball and falls in love with Cinderella. To "have a ball" means to have a lot of fun. The Fairy Godmother turns mice into horses and a pumpkin into a golden carriage. She "works her magic," which means to make something good happen. The Fairy Godmother also changes Cinderella's rags into a beautiful ball gown. Today, we use the saying "from rags to riches" to describe a poor person who becomes wealthy. A "fairy godmother" is someone who helps us in an unexpected way.

TALK ABOUT IT!

Like Cinderella, Isaac put his best foot forward. He brainstormed some sayings for his own fairy tale—from head to toe! He used an idiom dictionary to learn their meanings. Then he added the meanings to his chart.

HAVE YOUR HEAD IN THE CLOUDS
to daydream

GET IT OUT OF YOUR HAIR
to stop something from annoying you

HAVE A BIG HEAD
to be conceited

SCREAM YOUR HEAD OFF
to scream loudly

HAVE A GOOD MIND TO DO SOMETHING
to feel like you want to do something

HEAD AND SHOULDERS ABOVE
clearly better

HAVE YOUR NOSE IN THE AIR
to be stuck up or have a high opinion of yourself

A PAIN IN THE NECK
an annoyance

GIVE SOMEONE THE COLD SHOULDER
to ignore someone or treat them unkindly

BEHIND YOUR BACK
without you knowing

HAVE A CHANGE OF HEART
to change how you feel about something

COST AN ARM AND A LEG
cost a lot of money

TO HAVE A GUT FEELING
to sense what is the right thing to do

MAKE YOUR BLOOD BOIL
to make you feel really angry

SHAKE A LEG
to hurry

GET COLD FEET
to feel afraid when it's time to do something

WRITE ABOUT IT!

Isaac used the sayings he brainstormed to write a fine fairy tale. He underlined all the sayings in his story. Do some research yourself to find out what each one means.

Once upon a time, a <u>big-headed</u> prince named Robert ruled the land. He rode <u>on his high horse</u> with his <u>nose in the air</u>, and gave everyone <u>the cold shoulder</u>. The townspeople called him Snobby Bobby <u>behind his back</u>. Everyone wanted the snooty prince <u>out of their hair</u>. So a wizard locked him in a tall tower. Now the fate of the prince was really <u>up in the air</u>!

At first, Snobby Bobby thought the tower was a <u>pain in the neck</u>. His <u>blood boiled</u>, and <u>he screamed his head off</u>. Then the prince settled down and planned his escape. He <u>had a good mind to jump down to</u> the ground. He'd have to <u>shake a leg</u> before anyone saw him, but <u>he got cold feet</u>. Maybe he could tie his robes to the tower and climb down. But the robes <u>cost him an arm and a leg</u>. He didn't want to rip them.

Then Snobby Bobby had <u>a change of heart</u> and decided to stay in the high tower. Now he would always be <u>head and shoulders above the crowd</u>. And everyone in the land would have to <u>look up to him</u>! The townspeople were <u>on cloud nine</u> that the prince had his <u>head in the clouds</u>. And they <u>had a gut feeling</u> they would all live happily ever after.

NOW IT'S YOUR TURN!

Now it's your turn to use your head! Brainstorm some body sayings. Check their meanings online or in an idiom dictionary. Then use them to tell your fairy tale. Write about a dragon with a giant sweet tooth or a princess who puts her fancy foot in her mouth. Use your imagination, speak your mind, and break a leg!

SAYINGS IN FABLES

Now it's time to turn the tables and learn about **fables**! Fables are short stories used to teach **morals**, or lessons. They tell you to look before you leap. They teach you to never cry wolf or count your chickens before they're hatched. Many fables were written long ago by a man named Aesop. Over time, the morals of his stories have become proverbs and adages we use in everyday speech.

Read Aesop's fable about the crow and the pitcher below. See if you can guess a saying that came from the story. If you get it wrong, you won't have to eat crow!

THE CROW AND THE PITCHER

A thirsty Crow found a Pitcher with some water in it, but so little was there that, try as she might, she could not reach it with her beak, and it seemed as though she would die of thirst within sight of the remedy. At last she hit upon a clever plan. She began dropping pebbles into the Pitcher, and with each pebble the water rose a little higher until at last it reached the brim, and the knowing bird was enabled to quench her thirst.

DID THIS BIRD EAT CROW?

To be made to "eat crow" means having to admit to an embarrassing mistake. No, this saying did not come from this story.

The fable of the crow and the pitcher is filled to the brim with morals! Did you guess one of the sayings the story shows? Keep reading to find out if your answer holds water.

LITTLE BY LITTLE DOES THE TRICK.

This saying means you can achieve your goals in small steps. The crow dropped tiny stones into the pitcher, and "with each pebble the water rose a little higher." The bird was patient and took her time with the task. She did not stop "until at last it reached the brim." If the crow had used a large rock instead, she might have broken the pitcher—and hit rock bottom!

WHERE THERE'S A WILL, THERE'S A WAY.

This proverb means that if you really want to do something, you'll find a way to do it. The crow's task seemed impossible at first. "Try as she might," she could not quench her thirst. But the crafty crow didn't give up, and at last she found a way to get the water. It was just a stone's throw away!

NECESSITY IS THE MOTHER OF INVENTION.

This saying means that people invent things because they need to solve problems. The bird was dying of thirst when "she hit upon a clever plan." If she had not been so thirsty, the crow might have been a birdbrain and given up. Instead she was as wise as an owl and found a solution.

Have you ever had a lightbulb moment like the crow? That means you suddenly get a bright idea, like Thomas Edison did when he invented the light bulb. Without his brilliant invention, we might still be in the dark! Think of other inventions that solved problems and helped us move light-years ahead.

After reading about the thirsty crow, Sophia had a thirst for more proverbs! She decided to write a story that would teach her friends a lesson. She brainstormed some proverbs and adages she had heard before.

Gentle persuasion is better than force.
Slow and steady wins the race.
The early bird catches the worm.
Actions speak louder than words.
Two wrongs don't make a right.
Birds of a feather flock together.
Honesty is the best policy.
You can't teach an old dog new tricks.
A bird in the hand is worth two
    in the bush.
Don't judge a book by its cover.
Two heads are better than one.
Practice makes perfect.
The grass is always greener on the other side.

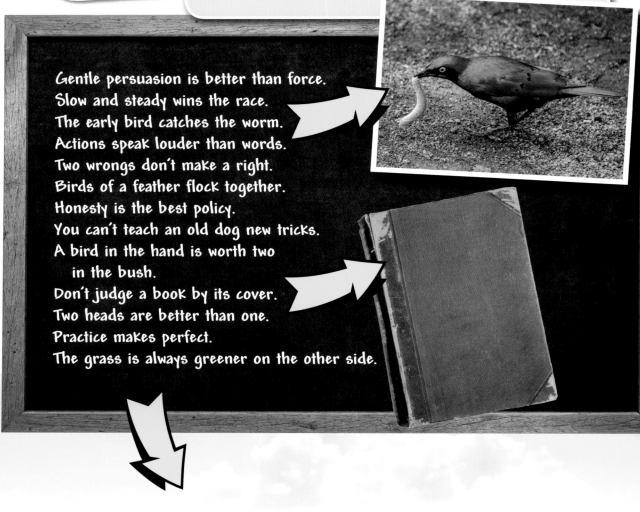

Sophia selected a saying for her story. She chose the proverb "slow and steady wins the race." In Aesop's fable, a slow but determined tortoise beats a quick and confident rabbit in a race. Sophia thought of ways to show that proverb in her own fable. She decided to tell a tale of three brothers eating spaghetti.

Three brothers sat down to eat some spaghetti. The oldest brother boasted that he could finish his food first. The middle brother argued that he would win the race. The little brother just bit his tongue, and started slurping his spaghetti. He knew his big brothers would have to eat their words.

Big brother dove into his spaghetti. Soon he was up to his ears in sauce! Then he spilled his milk all over the table in his rush to finish. His mom made him stop eating to clean it up. He was upset, but he didn't cry over spilled milk.

Meanwhile, middle brother was stuffing his face. He crammed noodle after noodle into his mouth. But he bit off more than he could chew. He choked on his spaghetti—and his boastful words! His dad made him stop eating to catch his breath.

Little brother just kept slurping his spaghetti little by little. He had a lot on his plate, but knew he could handle it. His brothers could only watch as little brother slowly but surely won the race. He grinned and served each of his brothers a big slice of humble pie.

SAY WHAT?

Did you spot another proverb in the story? "Don't cry over spilled milk" means to not get upset about things that can't be undone.

NOW IT'S YOUR TURN!

Now it's your turn to come to the table and write a fable! Use the proverb "two heads are better than one" to tell the tale of a two-headed monster. Write about an old dog that joins the circus and *does* learn new tricks. Or an early bird that catches a worm—and a bus—with some birds of a feather. Pick a proverb or add an adage, and teach your friends a thing or two.

SAYINGS IN MYTHS

Like fables, **myths** are ancient stories that have been told again and again. They are magical tales used to explain how the world works or how people should act. Over time, their stories and characters have magically turned into sayings we use today.

Achilles (pronounced uh-KIL-eez) was a mythical hero known for his strength and bravery. When he was a baby, his mother held him by the heels and dipped him in a magical river to protect him from harm. As an adult, he was killed in battle by an arrow to is heel. Today, a strong person's weakness is described as their "Achilles heel."

Pandora was a curious character who opened a forbidden box that held all the evils of the world. Today, the saying "opening Pandora's box" means to uncover problems you weren't expecting.

Midas was a greedy king who wished that everything he touched turned to gold. The gods granted him his wish—but be careful what you wish for!

Midas started up, in a kind of joyful frenzy, and ran about the room, grasping at everything that happened to be in his way. He seized one of the bedposts, and it became immediately a fluted golden pillar. He pulled aside a window curtain, in order to admit a clear spectacle of the wonders which he was performing; and the tassel grew heavy in his hand—a mass of gold. He took up a book from the table... Behold! it was a bundle of thin golden plates, in which all the wisdom of the book had grown illegible. He hurriedly put on his clothes, and was enraptured to see himself in a magnificent suit of gold cloth, which retained its flexibility and softness, although it burdened him a little with its weight.

—Excerpt from *The Golden Touch* by Nathaniel Hawthorne

In this passage, King Midas discovers that he's struck gold. Everything he touches turns into the precious metal. He joyfully runs around the room, changing bedposts, curtains, books, and clothes to gold. Today, we say that someone who succeeds at everything they do has "the Midas touch" or "the golden touch."

The Midas myth warns us, however, to be careful what you wish for—because you just might get it. That saying means that sometimes when you get what you want, it's not exactly what you expected. There are hints in this passage that King Midas's gift is really a curse. His golden book becomes unreadable and all its wisdom is lost. His robes turn into "a magnificent suit of gold cloth," but they hang heavily on him. Soon Midas's decision weighs heavily on him, too.

As the myth unfolds, King Midas is burdened more and more with his golden gift. He touches fragrant roses, and they harden and lose their scent. Tasty food turns to cold, hard metal when it touches his lips. In some versions of the myth, Midas hugs his daughter and she becomes a little statue with a heart of gold. In the end, the king regrets his greedy wish—and learns that "all that glitters is not gold."

TALK ABOUT IT!

Jason used the Midas myth as a model to write his own story. He hoped it would be fit for a king! He changed the story to a girl with a big sweet tooth. The girl wished that everything she touched turned to dessert. Jason used a story map to plan his sweet story. He wrote down notes for the beginning, middle, and end of his myth.

BEGINNING

There once was a girl who loved sweets.
She ate all kinds of desserts all day long.
She even had daydreams about them!

MIDDLE

A magic fairy visited the girl and offered her a wish.
The girl chose to turn everything she touched into something sweet.
She was like a kid in a candy store!

END

Soon the girl realized her sweet dream was a nightmare.
She started changing all her favorite toys into candy.
She begged the fairy to take the sweet spell away.

Jason added some details to sweeten his story. He named the main characters Candace (Candi for short) and the Sweet-Tooth Fairy. Then he sprinkled in some sayings for extra flavor. See if you can underline them yourself.

A girl named Candi had a giant sweet tooth. All day long she ate candy, ice cream, and pastries. She loved the way the cookies crumbled. She wanted to have her cake and eat it, too. She sweet-talked her friends and took their candy. She daydreamed about pie in the sky.

One day, the Sweet-Tooth Fairy visited Candi and offered her one wish. Candi wanted everything she touched to turn sugary sweet. She was like a kid in a candy store! She touched a carrot and it became carrot cake. It was a piece of cake! She touched a cherry and it turned into cherry pie. It was as easy as pie! Soon she had mountains of marshmallows and puddles of pudding.

But then things started to go wrong. Candi tried to ride her bike and the tires turned to jelly donuts. She squeezed her teddy bear, and it changed into a giant gummy bear. Her favorite things were becoming sweet nothings! Candi realized her wish was as nutty as a fruitcake. She begged the Sweet-Tooth Fairy to reverse her candy curse. Then she vowed to never eat sweets again—or at least for the rest of the afternoon.

NOW IT'S YOUR TURN!

Now it's your turn to do some sweet-talking! Use a myth as a model, but change the characters and plot to make it your own. Write a long story, or keep it short and sweet. Your friends will eat it up!

Keep reading to see how other students helped Jason revise his work.

REVISE YOUR WORK

You put your nose to the grindstone and learned some idioms, adages, and proverbs. You used the sayings to write all sorts of super stories. Now you'll learn how to polish your work so it shines like a new penny. Use this handy checklist to help you have your say with sayings.

RAISE YOUR VOICE

The words and sayings you use in your writing show the reader your **voice**. Voice is the unique personality of each writer. Using a catchy saying can make your writing funny or clever.

SAYINGS REVISION CHECKLIST

1. Did you tell an original story? You can include old sayings, but make sure your work is brand new.
2. Do the sayings make sense in your story? Make sure you check their meanings.
3. Were you careful not to use too many sayings? Some of the stories in this book are stuffed with sayings. Normally you wouldn't go overboard with them like that.
4. Did you avoid using too many clichés? Clichés are phrases or sayings that are overused and don't express original ideas.

PUT YOUR HEADS TOGETHER

You can revise your work by showing it to other students and picking their brains. They will put in their two cents and help you step up your game. And make no mistake about it, the students will also help you find spelling and grammar errors you missed. Remember that two heads are better than one—and three or four are even better!

MAKE IT BETTER

Jason shared his work with other students. They liked his story but had some ideas to make it even sweeter. Drew suggested that Candi dream of candy at night. His mom always wished him sweet dreams before bed, so maybe Jason could use that saying. Sophia thought he had too many clichés in his story. She suggested he cut the "piece of cake" or "easy as pie" sayings. Cassie thought it would be clever to say that things "went sour" instead of wrong, since the story was about sweets. Jason chewed on their suggestions for a while. Then he made a change for the better.

A girl named Candi had a giant sweet tooth. All day long she ate candy, ice cream, and pastries. She loved the way the cookies crumbled. She wanted to have her cake and eat it, too. She sweet-talked her friends and took their candy. She daydreamed about pie in the sky. At night she had sweet dreams of more sweets.

One day, the Sweet-Tooth Fairy visited Candi and offered her one wish. Candi wanted everything she touched to turn sugary sweet. She was like a kid in a candy store! She touched a carrot and it became carrot cake. She touched a cherry and it turned into cherry pie. Soon she had mountains of marshmallows and puddles of pudding. Making sweets was a piece of cake!

But then things started to go sour. Candi tried to ride her bike and the tires turned to jelly donuts. She squeezed her teddy bear, and it changed into a giant gummy bear. Her favorite things were becoming sweet nothings! Candi realized her wish was as nutty as a fruitcake. She begged the Sweet-Tooth Fairy to reverse her candy curse. Then she vowed to never eat sweets again—or at least for the rest of the afternoon.

PUBLISH YOUR WORK

The last piece of the puzzle—and the final step in the writing process—is publishing. Publishing means getting your work ready for an **audience**. An audience is all the people who see, read, or hear your work.

There are lots of ways to publish your pictures and stories. Draw a cartoon that makes your brother laugh his head off. Read a fairy tale to your knight in shining armor. Make an ancient myth as good as new, then teach your friends a lesson. Write the book on sayings and publish it online. Think big, or make a long story short. Just keep creating and spreading the word.

LEARNING MORE

BOOKS

In a Pickle And Other Funny Idioms by Marvin Terban. HMH Books for Young Readers, 2007.

Scholastic Dictionary of Idioms by Marvin Terban. Scholastic Reference, 2006.

Talking Turkey and Other Clichés We Say by Nancy Loewen. Picture Window Books, 2011.

There's a Frog in My Throat: 440 Animal Sayings a Little Bird Told Me by Loreen Leedy and Pat Street. Holiday House, 2004.

WEBSITES

Learning Games for Kids: Idioms
www.learninggamesforkids.com/vocabulary_games/idioms.html
These idiom games are more fun than a barrel of monkeys.

Mr. Nussbaum's Adages for Kids
http://mrnussbaum.com/idioms-for-kids/
Go to town with adages at this Adage Village website.

Mr. Nussbaum's Hungry Hangman Games
http://mrnussbaum.com/the-hungry-hangman-games-2/
If you're hungry for more sayings, try this hungry hangman proverb game.

Slime Kids Idiom Hunt
www.slimekids.com/games/literacy-games/idiom-hunt.html
Figure out the idiom, then choose the words in the correct order.

GLOSSARY

Note: Some boldfaced words are defined where they appear in the book.
brainstorm To think of many ideas, often in a group
burdened Weighed down by a heavy load
character A person, animal, or thing that interacts with others in a story
dialogue The words characters say in a story
illegible Not clear enough to read
moral A lesson learned from a story
novel A long book of fiction with characters and action
voice A writer's personality that shows in their word choices

INDEX

"**a** wolf in sheep's clothing" 11
adages 6, 20, 22
"ants in your pants" 8, 9
artwork 8–11
brainstorming 7, 10, 14, 18, 19, 22
candy story 26–27, 29
characters 6, 13, 15, 24, 27
clues to meanings 5, 8, 9, 11
drafting 7
editing 7
fables 20–23
fairy tales 16–19
figurative language 5, 8, 11
home stories 12–15
idioms 6, 8, 12, 16, 17, 18, 19
"**K**ing Midas" 24–25, 26
literal language 5, 8, 9, 11
"little by little does the trick" 21
morals 20–21
myths 24–28

"**n**ecessity is the mother of invention" 21
"**o**pen Pandora's box" 24
"opening a can of worms" 8, 9
proverbs 6, 20, 21, 22, 23
publishing 7, 30
"**r**aining cats and dogs" 8, 9
revising 7, 28–29
"**S**nobby Bobby "19
spaghetti story 23
steps to writing 7
stories 12–15
"**T**he Crow and the Pitcher" 20
"The Golden Touch" 24
"The History of Little Goody Two-Shoes" 12
"The Story of Cinderella" 16–17
visualizing 8
voice 28
"**w**hen pigs fly" 8, 9
"where there's a will, there's a way" 21
Wonderful Wizard of Oz, The 12–13